BRULÉ

HONOR AND LIFE Oil, 36 x 48 inches

BRULÉ

The Sioux People of the Rosebud

by PAUL DYCK

NORTHLAND PRESS / FLAGSTAFF, ARIZONA

To the Brulé Sioux People whose courage
and devotion to the land will live
forever in the hearts of free men everywhere

CONTENTS

FOREWORD

WHEN THE JOHN ANDERSON PHOTOGRAPHS were first shown to me by Carl Parlasca many years back, my first reaction was to immediately call my friend Paul Dyck. Parlasca had come into ownership of these historic glass plate negatives from Anderson's widow and was anxious for them to be recorded in book form for future generations. Both Paul and I were excited about the photographs and fortunately soon after Parlasca's friend Jack R. Williams of the United States Park Service came into possession of the plates, we were able to formulate plans for this book.

It is really unique in this era to find such a qualified man as Paul Dyck to edit the photographs, write the text and captions, as well as add the artistic and emotional strength needed to do justice to this priceless collection. Paul's love and knowledge of the Plains Indians came originally from reminiscences of his father who was an early pioneer in Calgary, Canada at the turn of the century and from the story of George Catlin, the early American artist who traveled among the Indians of the West. The young boy determined to continue the work Catlin had started in the 1830s. Thus, the enchantment with the remnants of the American Indian culture, begun in his early boyhood, developed into a continual lifelong dedication.

When Paul was still a small child he was taken to Europe, as part of the family tradition, for the study of art. Some years later, when he was fifteen and attending the Hagenbeck Circus in Europe, an incident occurred which was to have a profound effect on his life. It was there that he met One Elk, a Hunkpapa Sioux warrior veteran, priest and medicine man, who was a member of the circus troupe. Two years later Paul returned to the United States to be adopted into the family of One Elk who lived on the Grand River in South Dakota. One Elk was a veteran of the Custer

Battle and was one of the last of the so-called "Sitting Bull Boys," the elite warrior guard who surrounded Chief Sitting Bull during the Indian Wars period, and was present at Chief Sitting Bull's death in 1890. One Elk became Paul Dyck's spiritual guide and imparted to him knowledge that a warrior father gave a warrior son. He named him *Wi'-hun-ke E-ta'-pa,* "Rainbow Hand," for he felt the young man was able to paint the colors of the heavens.

The purposeful search for individuals and materials has rewarded Paul with life-long friendships among the people who were part of the history of the West: White Bull (possibly the man who killed Custer) and One Bull, both nephews of Chief Sitting Bull, Kills Enemy, Little Soldier, Judge Frank Zahn, Frank Kicking Bear, Respects Nothing, James Red Cloud, Horn Cloud – these are just a few of the personal contacts he has made. The search has led him among most of the tribes of the Plains and the names of friends and informants are legion since many were still alive in the middle 1930s. He has lived with other tribes such as the Cheyenne, Arapaho, Blackfeet, Crow, Pawnee, Oto, Kiowa, Comanche, Apache, Zuni, Hopi, and Navajo.

Pawnee Bill (Gordon W. Lillie), Mexican Joe, Ernest Thompson Seton, Walter Campbell (Stanley Vestal), Frederick "San Diego" Rawson, and Colonel Tim McCoy who is the last still active – all have helped to make his study of the Indian people more complete.

In the 1950s, Paul became the adopted son of Lone Wolf, the famous Blackfeet artist and sculptor and son of James Willard Schultz, author of the American classic *My Life as an Indian.* In 1970, Paul and Lone Wolf's widow Naoma carried his ashes to Montana to the ancestral burial grounds of Lone Wolf's family.

Paul Dyck has been privileged to study the American Indian of the West from the human as well as the ethnological viewpoint which enabled him to produce in the last forty years such paintings as the "Indians of the Overland Trail," a group of fourteen portraits which have been seen by more than four million people across the country.

With the publication of *Brulé,* an artist of international renown joins his vast and intimate knowledge of the American Indian with the rich legacy left by John Anderson, one of our great pioneer photographers, to make a significant contribution to the saga of the West.

PAUL E. WEAVER, JR.

PREFACE

THE SIOUX – Lakotas as they called themselves – created the romantic and heroic image of the American Indian. Their very existence affected most of the history of the Plains for they bore the brunt of the Indian Wars.

From the Platte River north to the Yellowstone, from the Missouri west to the Rocky Mountains stretched their domain of grasslands – a hunting paradise that developed the People into a special breed of men and created a culture that has become a national treasure of art and beauty.

With the return of the horse to the American scene, after several thousands of years of absence, the Plains People became a power to be reckoned with and an obstacle in the white man's march westward across the land. The planned destruction of the Indians' food supply – the buffalo – and then the advent of the reservation system hastened the end of this culture of freedom. To the white man, the Indian was a primitive savage who was not human; to the Indian, the white man was a godless creature and of a mentality confusing in its un-man-like behavior. The growing pains of the West wasted the best of both races – the best both peoples had to offer. It is only now, long afterwards, that we can and should gain inspiration from the early men who were the makers of America.

If there ever will be a time when we shall recognize that the People of the Plains were American patriots and heroes, our history books will have to be rewritten from a new viewpoint on humanity relative to our Constitution and the Bill of Rights, for throughout the trying historical period of westward expansion, the Indians of the West never lost their allegiance to America.

Brown Hat's "Winter Count History" of the Brulé Sioux People records the event of the winter of 1762-63 as the year that named these people of the Sioux Nation. The tribe was camped on the shore of a lake in eastern South Dakota when a prairie fire caught them. Some were burned to death out on the prairie. Those who did manage to save themselves by leaping into the waters of the lake had their legs and thighs badly burned by the fire, which resulted in scars. From that time on, this tribe was called *Sichangu* or "Burned Thighs" by all the Sioux. The early French traders translated this to "Brulé," a name soon to be recognized in the history of the white man's occupation of the West.

The Brulé, followed by the Oglala People, were the first of the Sioux Nation to reach the Great Plains of the West. The rest of the seven tribes of the nation stayed east of the Missouri River until, pressed by the ever-increasing occupation of their lands by the white man, they moved, one by one, onto the prairies of the West.

From the autumn of 1804, when Lewis and Clark met the Brulé at the mouth of the Bad River, until the time of the Wounded Knee Massacre, the Brulé People left an imprint on the history of the West that can be matched only by a very few. The People provided many national heroes whose devotion to the land matched their willingness to give their hearts and their blood for the sake of freedom. Outstanding historical individuals such as Brave Bear, Spotted Tail, Two Strike, and many others gave to the Brulé People heroes who are cherished and honored by the descendants of the warriors today.

This book is a record of the Brulé People during their transition from free men of the Plains to ragged prisoners of the reservation system, and is possibly the most complete record of photographs of that period ever taken. It brings reality to events that took place over eighty years ago. From the Treaty of Laramie in 1868 up to the present time, the changes in their way of life which these Americans saw and lived through – still maintaining some degree of identity – have become one of the epics for survival of the human race.

The man seen here was a man who knew the value of freedom; a man who walked and lived with God; a man whose eyes needed beauty as a way of life. Come then with me and join these men who have just come in from the mountains and the prairies. Come and rub shoulders with these men who have made the history of the West and who live again in this book of the Brulé People.

PAUL DYCK

THE JOHN ANDERSON PHOTOGRAPHS

from the Jack R. Williams Collection

CHAPTER 1

THE ROSEBUD AGENCY

BY THE 1850s the situation in the West along the Immigrant Trail to California and Oregon had deteriorated to the point that the Indian Tribes of the Plains had to be contained and removed if the march westward was to continue. By a number of solemn treaties between the United States government and the tribes of the Plains, the Sioux tribes being the most powerful at the time, the process of removal began.

The first attempt to keep the peace began with promises of food and trade goods; however, the food and the trade goods reached only a few of the People involved and the policy was a failure. With the Treaty of Laramie the hunting grounds were lost and the removal of the People to designated agencies was started. The treaty payments were to be given out only at the designated agencies and the Indian tribes were forced to move to the agencies or starve. Thus the reservation system was born.

The Brulé People were moved five times before Rosebud Agency was established as a permanent location. Whetstone Agency, Whiteriver Agency, Spotted Tail Agency (close to Camp Sheridan), Ponca Agency – all were disastrous to the morale and health of the People. Finally, through the efforts of Chief Spotted Tail, the Rosebud Reservation and Agency was established in the spring of 1878.

To the Indian people the reservation system was a tragedy and a prison. To live by a system which forced them to stay in one locality was unthinkable. Their way of life had disappeared and the new way of the white man was a sad replacement and one that could not be understood.

With the buffalo gone, the Great Plains were no longer the hunting paradise of the Indian people. It was a lonely place, full of memories of happiness. At the agency, the People became beggars, dispirited and hopeless, dirty and sick. The replacement of the *tipi* (tepee) with the white man's log house was the strangest of all. Some of the People thought that this was the white man's idea for killing them off that much faster. To the white authorities, however, the log house, with all its disadvantages to the Indian, became a symbol of their success in civilizing the Indian people.

The white man kept insisting that his way was the only way; that it was much better and it was the blessed way! The Indian people of the early reservation period could not see the "Promised Land" nor understand the "Promised Light." Out of the desperation caused by starvation and the starkness of the reservation system, the new religion of the Ghost Dance came as a salvation from this misery and ended in the tragic Wounded Knee Massacre.

Political upheavals and the lack of congressional appropriations made fulfillment of treaty obligations to the Indian people an almost impossible task. There were sincere and able agency men who tried – and tried honestly – but the gulf between the red man and the white man was not to be bridged easily. Practically none of the agency men had enough experience with the Indian way of life to make this new system palatable to the Indian people – a people whose own way of life was several thousand years in its development and who could not comprehend the change taking place in just a few short years. The old wise men of the People used to say that the white man could not possibly like his chiefs very much as he was constantly changing them.

The beauty of life for the Indian people was gone. It was only in the nostalgic memories of the Old Ones that remnants of the culture survived, to be cherished by the children of a different world.

Early tipi village on the Rosebud Reservation. With the buffalo gone, the old skin lodges disappeared and trade canvas took the place of buffalo hide for the tipis.

Rosebud Agency, 1889. The center of all government activities; the Indian agent's office and home; the army and Indian police headquarters; the supply depot; the trading post, center of the white man's civilization — the new way of life. There were over five thousand Brulé People registered on the agency rolls at this time.

A gathering of the People at the old Jordan Trading Post for a council in 1889. Wagons were taken along in expectation of rations to be issued by the government.

Nº 267. INDIAN CELEBRATION.
PHOTO BY J. A. ANDERSON.

Indians and United States Commissioners holding a council at Rosebud Agency, May 4, 1889. The council, headed by General Crook, was held in front of the log house of Louis Roubideaux, the interpreter, who was half French and half Indian. His house adjoined the Jordan Trading Post.

Indian police guard, escorting the Indian agent from Valentine, Nebraska, to Rosebud Agency. The annuity payments by the government to the Indians (usually in silver dollars) were sent by railroad to Valentine and then taken overland by wagon to the agency.

Rosebud Indian police, 1895, standing before their quarters. Stationed at different parts of the reservation which, at that time, constituted four counties. Many old-time warriors were chosen for this job on the reservation since their own society standing commanded respect and this made the law and order problems easier for the government. Their appointment undermined the power of the chiefs by putting all the authority in the hands of the white agents.

Rosebud Agency had sixty policemen. Half were kept on duty at the agency; the other half policed the outside camps. The enlisted men received ten dollars per month and the officers received fifteen to thirty dollars per month. Each man was expected to furnish his own horse.

Indian Police Force, Rosebud Agency SD

*Company of soldiers occupying the Rosebud
Agency during the Ghost Dance Outbreak
in 1890 which resulted in the Wounded
Knee Massacre. Serving as protection for
the agency, they had lookouts posted all
over the surrounding hills.*

The Jordan Trading Post in 1893. This building replaced the old log building which had burned down the previous year.

A special occasion preceding a celebration on pay day at the Jordan Trading Post.

Interior of the new trading post, 1893, before the large front room was added. Men gathered to talk over the problems of the world. The bottles labeled "Painkiller Medicine" on the back shelf, and the notice, "Don't sit on Counter or Floor," were signs of the times.

Enlarged interior of the trading post, show-
ing the different trade goods available
to the Indian people. The business volume
of this small trading post was great when
one considers that the annuity payments
to the Indians amounted to as much as
$150,000. Much of this money ended up
here in exchange for goods handed
over the counter.

The horse carriage of U. S. Indian Agent, James G. Wright, 1890. He was very proud of this outfit and was an expert with four-in-hand driving. The buffalo coat on the man next to the carriage was typical winter clothing in the Dakotas.

Ox teams hauled all freight to the agency from the nearest railroad depot at Valentine, Nebraska, a forty-mile trip. Firewood was hauled long distances as little was available near the agency. When annuity payments were made, the wagons hauled goods day and night — goods needed and not needed — until the Indian people had spent all their money.

Under the guidance of different religious groups, schools were established on the reservation. One job of the Indian police was to see that children were not hidden away and that they attended school. This photograph was taken to show the government officials the progress made — from long hair and blanket — after four years of schooling under Episcopalian guidance.

chief spotted tail

SPOTTED TAIL, known to the Indians as *Sinte Galeska,* was the most important Brulé chief during the turbulent period of the Indian Wars and of the early reservation period. He was possibly the greatest man the Brulé Nation ever produced. Born in 1823, this date is noted in his own affidavit of 1878. His father, Tangle Hair, and his mother, Walks with the Pipe, had several other children besides Spotted Tail. His boyhood name was Jumping Buffalo, but he acquired his warrior name of Spotted Tail after he was given a racoon tail by a friendly white trapper. The tail became his "medicine" or good-luck charm in battle and he was seen wearing it in his headdress by the soldiers at Fort Laramie in the 1850s. His two sisters married the Oglala medicine man, Crazy Horse, the father of the famous Oglala war chief, Crazy Horse of Custer Battle fame.

Spotted Tail's first war experience was against the Pawnees. He was sixteen and was a scout for a war party along with several other young men. Between the years of 1835 and 1855 his warrior record included one hundred scalps and he gained the rank of a war-shirt wearer. He still had the scalp-decorated shirt in his possession as late as 1870.

By 1866, Spotted Tail was clearly the head chief of the Brulé People. The following years, fraught with the troubles that brought the Custer Battle, found Spotted Tail more prominent in the governmental dealings with the Brulé Sioux. Because of the lack of sufficient cooperation in 1877 on the part of Red Cloud, the chief of the Oglalas, General Crook appointed Spotted Tail as the head chief of both his own people, the Brulés, and of the Oglalas.

As a leader of several delegations to Washington, D.C., Spotted Tail obtained more importance and experience in his dealings with the white man and with the United States government. The dissension within the tribe, encouraged by the government, the religious factions of the white man, and the total control of the reservation system contributed to the destruction of tribal life as the People once knew it, and produced a time that was ripe for the final curtain on the tragedy that took place August 5, 1881, the assassination of Spotted Tail by Crow Dog, himself a Brulé.

Spotted Tail was assassinated when he was leaving a council where he had again been elected to represent the Brulé Sioux in a delegation to Washington. The first to reach the scene of the murder were chiefs He Dog, Two Strike, and Ring Thunder.

The causes for the assassination are obscure. Personal rivalry was probably more responsible than anything else. There is no question, however, that the political situation within the tribe, inflamed by outside interest, was greatly responsible. The rivalry between the Progressives, headed by Spotted Tail, and the Non-Progressives or "Blanket Indians," headed by Two Strike, created an explosive situation. Crow Dog was one of the first, after Chief Swift Bear, to sign away the Sioux land in the Land Commissions Council in 1889. This definitely puts him on the side of the Progressives who were willing to cooperate with the government.

Some say that the assassination was the result of a blood feud between Crow Dog and Spotted Tail dating back to 1869 when Spotted Tail killed Crow Dog's friend, Big Mouth. Big Mouth, opposed to the chieftancy of Spotted Tail, had encouraged the whiskey trade to the Brulés. Spotted Tail, known for his distaste for whiskey and seeing the eventual destruction of his people by alcohol, defied Big Mouth. The killing occurred when, after an all-day drinking bout, Big Mouth tried to provoke a fight with Spotted Tail. He drew a gun on him but the gun misfired; Spotted Tail then shot and killed him.

There may have been other factors involved – both personal and political – but with Spotted Tail's death, the Brulé People's tribal structure ended and only little voices were heard from then on. No one individual could gather the People's support which Spotted Tail had held as a chief. Two Strike became the chief. He tried bravely to carry on and hold the People together against the confusing world that had descended upon them.

*Spotted Tail. The photograph was taken by
Alexander Gardner in Washington, D.C.,
1872.*

Spotted Tail and Fast Bear at Fort Laramie, Wyoming, 1868. One of the earliest photographs of Spotted Tail attributed to Alexander Gardner. Spotted Tail chose Fast Bear, a head warrior, to accompany him on the first journey to Washington in 1870 to see President Ulysses S. Grant.

Spotted Tail and wife, date unknown. The presence of the Andrew Johnson Peace Medal would indicate the date being between 1865 and 1871. These medals were given to the head chief of the Indian tribes as a token of friendship. Spotted Tail had five wives during his life and about thirty-four children. Few survived long. In 1940 only three grandchildren were alive out of this once large family.

Spotted Tail by Alexander Gardner, taken in Washington, D.C. This photograph was possibly used as a model for the well-known painting of Spotted Tail by the artist, H. Ulke, in 1877.

Spotted Tail with his children at Carlisle,
Pennsylvania in 1880. Seated left to right:
Stays at Home (William), age 18; Chief
Spotted Tail; Little Scout (Pollock), age 9.
Standing: Talks with Bear (Oliver), age 14;
Bugler (Max), age 12.

*Crow Dog was of the Orphan Band of the
Brulé People and was nephew of the head
Brulé chief, Brave Bear, who was killed
in the Grattan Fight in 1854. A proven
warrior, Crow Dog felt that the chieftainship
should have been left in the Brave Bear
family. As one of the Brulé soldiers who
escorted Crazy Horse to Fort Robinson
(after Crazy Horse came to the Brulé Agency
and before he was to surrender to the army),
Crow Dog was present at the arrest and
killing of Crazy Horse. Agent Cicero Newell
appointed Crow Dog as his chief of police,
a position that caused trouble between
Spotted Tail and Crow Dog.*

CHIEF SPOTTED TAIL **45**

Crow Dog was arrested for killing Spotted
Tail and tried in Deadwood, South Dakota.
He was condemned to hang but was released
after a decision was handed down by the
Supreme Court that civilian authorities
did not have jurisdiction over Indian affairs.
Crow Dog returned to Rosebud and the
loss of Spotted Tail, the Brulé's most able
chief, proved only that, under the new way
of life, one Sioux could kill another.

CROW DOG

Spotted Tail's "white man's" house, built in 1880. The government project of teaching the Sioux to live in white man's houses was thought to succeed better if houses were built for the different head chiefs, thus setting an example for the common people. It was said by the people opposed to Spotted Tail that the house cost the government $40,000, a figure much exaggerated even by the standards of the time.

CHAPTER 3

The People

THE OLD WAY OF LIFE was gone, yet the fire of remembrance was in the face of each proud warrior, men who were removed only by a few years from the din of the battle for the survival of their land. These were men of honor, men in step with God and His creation, men whom only this unique culture could produce.

These portraits show the beauty and art of the Brulé culture during a time when heirlooms still could be seen and were used – heirlooms that were very much alive in the eyes of the People. This was a time when all the People were still conscious of their need for beauty, a time when art was a part of every individual and not just an inanimate object without the pulse of life to be seen in a museum case.

The Indians of the Plains created the finest examples of classic beauty and elegance. Their heritage of beauty, an Indian people's legacy to all Americans, was born here as the only true native art and was created by a people not affected by other un-related cultures. The invention of the decorative use of porcupine quillwork, where the quills were dyed with natural dyes and sewn on buckskin with sinew, was a unique American first, duplicated nowhere else in the world. In comparing the old quilled pieces of art with later pieces decorated with the trade-introduced beads, the difference becomes self-evident; beadwork was merely an easier substitute in the trying periods of the Indian Wars when time was of the essence and life was under continuous harassment.

The art that the People of the Plains created was in complete harmony with nature and was always inspired by nature. Natural in beauty as any human, animal, or bird form created by God, it was therefore a perfect example of classical proportion and color, and yet it was completely functional for the everyday life of the People.

What beauty must have been seen by the eyes of the early explorers such as Lewis and Clark – a beauty that was to be denied its very existence because of political and religious reasons of conquest. How unsuccessfully, in his own time, did the great American artist George Catlin labor in the 1830s to make the American people conscious of the art treasures of the West. America had only deaf ears and blind eyes for this kind of beauty and George Catlin had to turn elsewhere in the world – to Europe – to find appreciation for the art and life he saw out on the western Plains.

By the 1880 period the art had begun to disappear. The white man's culture was overwhelming the native art. It was being stamped out, in some cases, by force. Its creation did at times bring imprisonment to the individuals by the Indian agents.

Many fine examples of the classical art of the Plains were collected by a handful of individuals and are now preserved in the museums of America. It was the far-sightedness of these men and their belief in the greatness of the native American art that has saved this glimpse of a once great culture for the future generations. These collections, however, have been ignored by the public and by the educational systems who have consistently promoted and continue to promote anything and everything as long as it wasn't created in America.

The ill-fitting and the ill-appearing "white man's" apparel was a sad substitute for the elegance of the old way. One has but to look to realize the magnitude of the loss to American culture which was thrown away by the misguided and the ignorant.

The smell of buffalo, the grass, the campfire, and the joy of the freedom of the land –the eyes, hands and heart that once, not long ago, knew a life that was full and good. These are the memories etched on the faces of the men and women who lived and witnessed the battle for the West.

All the important Brulé leaders on the Rosebud Reservation attending the council of
the Sioux Land Commission in May, 1889.
The Commission, headed by General Crook,
forced the Sioux to sign away nine million
acres of their land. At the extreme left is
Louis Roubideaux, the official interpreter
who was of French and Indian blood.
C. P. Jordan, the trader, is on the extreme
right. Front row, from the left: Tall Man,
Turning Eagle, Thin Elk, Big Head, Picket
Pin, Turning Bear, High Bear, Lance, High
Pipe, High Hawk, Yellow Hair, Little Thun-
der, Bear Head, He Dog, and Black Bull.
Back row, from the left: Louis Roubideaux,
Whirlwind Soldier, Yellow Horse, Good
Voice, White Crane Walking, Pretty Eagle,
Blue Eyes, Ring Thunder, Big Horse,
Stranger Horse, Quick Bear, Blunt Arrow,
Swift Bear, Poor Dog, Good Voice, Jr.,
Hollow Horn Bear, Crow Dog, Two Strike,
Milk, Sky Bull, Stands and Looks Back,
Bear Looks Behind, and C. P. Jordan.

Chief Two Strike, born in 1821, was in his younger years a warrior with Spotted Tail. By his own statement, his name came from a hunting incident when he was sixteen. He shot one arrow killing two buffalo cows — the arrow went through one cow and hit another, killing both. He had two sons and two daughters. He died in 1914.

Chief Two Strike, 1896. The use of a common trade axe instead of a tomahawk was popular and it was usually decorated in the same manner.

No 213. TWO-STRIKE. SIOUX CHIEF.
PHOTO. & COPYRIGHT. BY- J.A. ANDERSON. 1896.

Chief Two Strike. Stone-headed war clubs
were war relics, and being heirlooms by this
time, were used more for sentimental reasons.

When Two Strike was very old he used to come to the agency with his buggy and team, his prized possession, which he considered the most important mark of his rank even though he was a Non-Progressive chief.

Chief Two Strike with Bullman in the center and Little Hawk on the right. Little Hawk has Two Strike's American flag over his shoulder and is bringing it to a celebration.

Chief Two Strike's Camp, located between Rosebud Agency and St. Francis Catholic Mission School. This was a progressive camp for the times, with most of the People already living in log houses.

No. 252 MODERN INDIAN VILLAGE.
Photo by J. A. Anderson.

*Four generations of the Two Strike family.
Old Chief Two Strike is holding his great-
grandson; the son on the right and the
grandson are holding the American flag
of which the old chief was very proud.
The photograph was taken in 1914
just before his death.*

Chief Iron Shell, born in the 1820s, was the
son of one of the principal Brulé chiefs
in the 1840s. He was a prominent warrior,
along with Spotted Tail, as early as 1840.

Sioux Chief Iron Shell.
Copyright 1900.
By J. A. Anderson.

Chief Hollow Horn Bear, son of Chief Iron Shell. General Drum, who was then a lieutenant in the Bluewater Fight with the Brulés under General Harney in 1855, found a child on the battlefield after the fight. He returned it to the Brulés. This child was Iron Shell's son, Hollow Horn Bear.

Chief Hollow Horn Bear. A great orator
and a man interested in the affairs of the people.
Invited by President Theodore Roosevelt
for his inauguration, he was also present
at President Woodrow Wilson's. While in
Washington, D.C., he contracted pneumonia
and died. His body was shipped back to
Rosebud Reservation in 1913.

Chief Hollow Horn Bear. His portrait is on the old 14¢ U.S. postage stamp and the old $5 currency bills.

The girl at the extreme left in the back row
is the daughter of Chief Hollow Horn Bear.
She is wearing a blanket with a beaded strip.

The other six sons of old Chief Iron Shell;
Hollow Horn was not present in this photo-
graph and two of the sons are not identified
by name. Back row center: Peter Iron Shell;
front row seated from the left: Old Bear
Dog, He Frightens, and Pretty Bird.

Pretty Bird, son of old Chief Iron Shell.

Old Bear Dog, oldest surviving son of Chief Iron Shell, who was still living in 1935.

*Chief High Hawk, historian of the Brulé
People. His father, Brown Hat, born in 1821
or 1822, known as Battiste Good, kept a
historical record of the People which the
Sioux called a "Winter Count." Each year
was a symbol representing some outstanding
happening of that particular year. The record
began with the year 1700 and was carried
on by Brown Hat until the year 1880. He
was able to put down a historical record
from the information gained by talking
to the oldest Brulés. The actual date of
creating the "Winter Count" is unknown;
however, it is possible it was created by
Brown Hat as late as 1863. Chief High
Hawk carried on with the record.
He is holding a silver headed presentation
cane given to the various chiefs by
President Abraham Lincoln as a
badge of a chief's office.*

CHIEF HIGH HAWK
COPYRIGHT 1900
BY J. A. ANDERSON.

Chief High Hawk and his three wives
and children. His son, Young High Hawk,
is at the extreme right.

Young High Hawk who became well known
because of the photographs of
Edward S. Curtis in the classic,
"North American Indian."

Chief He Dog, the brother warrior of Chief Crazy Horse and the constant companion of Crazy Horse throughout the battles and fights of the Indian Wars, from the Grattan Fight at Fort Laramie in 1854 to Crazy Horse's death at Fort Robinson in 1877. He Dog put his own red blanket over his dying brother-friend when he was killed after surrendering to the army. After the body was released to the parents of Crazy Horse, the old father, also named Crazy Horse, along with He Dog, quietly took the remains to a secret burial place. He then established his camp with the Spotted Tail people and, as late as 1881, Old Crazy Horse maintained his camp west of the agency. Later the camp came to be known as the He Dog Camp. In 1880, Spotted Tail took Iron Wing with him as a representative of the surrendered hostiles from Old Crazy Horse's Camp on his trip to Carlisle and Washington. Chief He Dog was born around 1830 in Old Smoke's Camp on the Laramie Plains. He was a nephew of Chief Red Cloud, his mother being Red Cloud's sister. His younger brother, Short Bull, brought the Ghost Dance to the Brulé Sioux after journeying to Nevada to see the prophet, Wovoka. He Dog died in 1931 at Pine Ridge, South Dakota, at the age of 101.

Chief He Dog's daughter, the oldest girl holding the horse, with young relatives.

Chief Swift Bear, son of Lone Dog, was, by 1865, the second ranking chief of the Brulés. Born in the 1820s, Swift Bear was a contemporary of Chief Spotted Tail. He was the second to sign the Treaty of 1866 as a chief of the Corn Band of the Brulé. Together with Chief Spotted Tail, he was a ranking member of the first Brulé delegation to Washington, D.C., in 1870. His sister was married to James Bordeaux, the trader from St. Louis who came to Fort Laramie country sometime in the 1840s. Swift Bear, a peace chief, quickly adopted the white man's way of life. In 1889, he was one of the first to sign away the Sioux lands at a council headed by General Crook and the Sioux Land Commission.

Turning Bear. Indicted and tried for the murder of a Nebraska citizen in 1880, he was not held because the civilian authorities did not have legal power over Indians, setting a precedent for the release of Crow Dog after his trial for the assassination of Spotted Tail. During the Ghost Dance Outbreak in 1890-91, Turning Bear was one of the leading dancers.

TURNING BEAR.
SIOUX WARRIOR.
COPYRIGHT 1900. J.A. ANDERSON

*Turning Bear and wife. Turning Bear sent
his son to Carlisle School in Pennsylvania
for three years. As he went to meet the boy
upon his return from school, he was killed
by a railroad train at Valentine, Nebraska.
This event was recorded on Kills Two's
"Winter Count" historical record as
the "Winter of 1912."*

A young man with a perfect example of an old heirloom shirt. It is trimmed with porcupine quills, ermine skins, and scalp locks taken from an enemy.

A mother and her three daughters wearing the typical reservation day dress of the 1890 period. Dresses of trade cloth, decorated with elk teeth, were highly prized by the womenfolk.

Five generations of women in one family.

Two women, both ninety years old, who never married and who lived together until they died. It was very unusual for Indian women not to marry.

*Oldest woman of the Brulé People in 1910.
She was then over 100 years old, according
to her own "Winter Count" which
she kept up.*

Picket Pin. This man was accused of dis-
mantling the log houses of the Ghost Dancers
who had left their homes and of selling
the wood to the white settlers. Many Ghost
Dancers burned their houses themselves
as an act of defiance and disregard
for the new way of life.

No. 915
PICKET-PIN. "SIOUX"
COPYRIGHT 1900
BY J. A. ANDERSON.

*Picket Pin, wearing an old-time Sioux
winter cap made of fur.*

Picket Pin, with his family and house. His wife, on the left, is wearing a sacred porcupine-quilled buffalo robe. These were worn only by very virtuous and honored people.

No. 271. PICKET PIN AND FAMILY
PHOTO BY: J.A. ANDERSON

Charlie Picket Pin, son of Old Picket Pin,
dressed up for a dance. A rejected lover, he
tried to commit suicide by shooting himself.
Unfortunately, he only succeeded in putting
out his eye. From that time on, he wore
a cloth over the empty eye socket.

Chief Quick Bear of the Black Pipe District.
His son Ruben was one of the first Sioux
boys to enter Carlisle School in Pennsylvania.

A group of young Brulé Sioux men and a woman in the finest clothing, 1897. The woman was a survivor of the Wounded Knee Massacre. She lived for eight years after the battle, dying finally from the wounds she had received at the time. The man at the right wearing an eagle feather bonnet is Plenty Horses, the Carlisle School graduate who killed Lieutenant Casey during the Ghost Dance Outbreak. William Eagle Bird, seated at the right of the woman, was still alive in 1940. This group photograph shows some of the best examples of the development of Brulé art and elegance.

A family group in the "Sunday" clothes imposed upon them by the new way of life. Compare these with the dress in the preceding photograph. To the Indian the white man's clothes were not very beautiful – something incomprehensible to the early white educators.

Eagle Pipe, one of the survivors of the Custer Battle, wearing an old grizzly-claw necklace, an item highly prized by the warriors of the Plains. Eagle Pipe was one of the men who threw Agent Wright out of his office during a mob action inside the building, an incident involving several hundred of the Brulé Sioux. The riot, which nearly got out of control, was caused by Chief Wooden Knife's complaint about the agent's distribution of the treaty goods.

920
EAGLE PIPE "SIOUX"
COPYRIGHT 1900
BY J.A.ANDERSON.

Little Bald Eagle, wearing a war shirt of the traditionally classic pattern. It is trimmed with scalp locks and porcupine quills. These shirts, highly valued by the warriors, were either buried with their owners or handed down to the descendants.

LITTLE BALD EAGLE
COPYRIGHT BY J.A.ANDERSON. 1903.

Little Bald Eagle with his family. This family was well-to-do because of a steady income from the son who was employed with the Indian police.

Chief Stands and Looks Back. A veteran of the Custer Battle, relative of Chief Red Cloud, and the brother of Trader C. P. Jordan's wife. His war shirt is richly decorated with porcupine quillwork. The quilled strip on the trade cloth blanket was very unusual at this time.

Sarah Blue Eyes. She was the wife of Trader C. P. Jordan and the daughter of Old Sarah Blue Eyes who also had blue eyes. This was a rarity among the full bloods and was caused by a lack of pigmentation at birth. The elks-tooth dress was a great prestige item among the Indian women. The German silver concho belt was a trade item purchased from the white traders.

*One Star, wearing a bandolier of bone
pipes, a trade item, and a favorite decoration
for both men and women.*

No 916.
ONE STAR. SIOUX.
COPYRIGHTED 1900
BY J.A.ANDERSON

One Star and his spotted pony, his great pride. Most of the warriors' horses were highly prized and were trained either for war or for the hunt.

Fool Bull, medicine man and warrior, holding his old battle shield with a decorated cover and a horse quirt of a special type — a symbol of the Dog Soldier Society. The quirt was probably made out of pinewood moulding from a white man's house.

Eagle Man, a medicine man. The canvas shirt was a holdover from the Ghost Dance. Most of the People threw the shirts away after they failed to protect them from the soldiers' bullets.

931
EAGLE MAN.
COPYRIGHT 1900.
BY J. A. ANDERSON

Eagle Man, holding a carved wooden gun which was decorated with scalps taken in battle when he was a young man.

EAGLE MAN,
"SIOUX"

COPYRIGHT 1900.
BY J.A.ANDERSON.

Bear Stands Up. The old warrior is wearing his Sun Dance whistle which is made from an eagle bone. This was a symbol that he had participated in a real Sun Dance in the time before the complete ceremony was forbidden by the government authorities.

928.
BEAR STANDS UP.
COPYRIGHT 1900. J. A. ANDERSON.

High Horse, Chief of the Cutmeat District, with his fine porcupine-quilled war shirt. He is holding his pipe and eagle-wing fan and knows that he is beautiful. A comparison of the costume in this portrait and that of Good Voice may help to explain the impoverishment felt by the Indians — a people who loved beauty — when they were forced to adopt the white man's culture.

917
Sioux Chief High Horse
Copyright 1900.
By J.A. Anderson

Good Voice, one of the first to adopt white man's dress. He was termed a good "progressive" Indian by the agency authorities.

SIOUX CHIEF GOOD VOICE
PHOTO BY J.A. ANDERSON.

Stranger Horse, wearing two Peace Medals.
This was a very unusual habit as the medals
were very highly valued at this time and were
most likely obtained through inheritance.

Old Harney, an Indian Scout for General Harney from whom he got his name. He scouted for the army in the early campaign of 1855 in the Platte and Fort Laramie Districts.

OLD HARNEY,
COPYRIGHT 1900
BY J.A.ANDERSON

Old Harney, wearing the old-time fur hat. This type of apparel was rarely seen in the reservation period. The grizzly-claw necklace around his neck is of unusual size. Harney was 100 years old when this photograph was taken.

Old Harney's Camp. Old Harney and his grandson are in the foreground. By this time, the white man's goods — wagons, trunks, kettles — were the standard equipment of all the camps on the Rosebud.

Yellow Hair and his wife. In 1870, he was chosen by Swift Bear to accompany him and Spotted Tail in the delegation to Washington, D.C., to see President Grant. This was the first Brulé delegation to make the journey. In 1880-81, a faction of the Brulé chiefs opposed to Spotted Tail's policies supported Yellow Hair as a replacement to Spotted Tail.

YELLOW HAIR & WIFE
COPYRIGHT 1900.
BY J.A. ANDERSON

Little Hawk in white man's clothing. He is still wearing his hair in fur wraps which was a custom of the old-time warriors.

A group of chiefs who have come in for a council with Agent Covey. This was taken in front of the old office building at the agency. Chief Two Strike is in the front row, third from the left.

CHAPTER 4

AGENCY LIFE

COUNTLESS BOOKS have been written on the subject but no words can compare with the actual picture by an eye witness who was there. The confusion and the newness of the white man's road was ever present. Yet when the long-horned cattle, the "humpless buffalo of the white man," arrived at the agency after having been driven all the way from Texas under government and army contracts, the old spark of the buffalo hunter of a thousand years came to life. "Red meat, red meat! People, come! Life is good again!" The fact that the Texas cattle were but skin and bones was not noted by eyes brimming with the tears of memory.

The strangeness of the goods of the white culture was at its height. Many of the items were to be seen and tasted for the first time. No longer could a man go out and support his family by the hunt. Now he had to beg – beg for what supposedly was his own, given to him by treaty rights. Once the country was bountiful and the buffalo limitless. The new philosophy of life – the white man's life, where man, not God, would put limits on the food and life needs – this was beyond the understanding of the Wise Ones and life was not beautiful anymore. The old pride was gone and the grayness of poverty and misery took over. Just once in awhile, a flash of the old appeared in some costume item mixed with the rags of trade goods which, unlike the old buckskin, could not stand the harshness of the country.

Sickness upon sickness was brought upon the People by the new way of never changing the location of the camp and the life in airless log houses. The medical facilities of the agencies being inadequate at best, the old medicine men unable to cope with the new diseases, the People were nearly decimated to the point of extinction.

The agricultural ideas of the new system did not appeal at all. To plow up grassy

soil that had sustained life for countless generations and then watch it blow away
– this did not make sense. The white man must be a fool, his way a fool's road.

Yet . . . somehow, the Sioux survived the despair and adversity of the early
agency days and retained his pride in being an American.

*A tipi camp of the Brulé Sioux, taken in
1890, during the Ghost Dance excitement.*

The change of living – from the tipi to the log house – took a long time. The People still preferred the tipi, even in the severe Dakota winters, since the log houses caused them to sicken and die.

To visit with friends and relatives was, and still is, one of the great joys of all the People.

White Thunder's Camp, north of the agency, 1889. Here, at this camp in 1884, young Spotted Tail, son of Chief Spotted Tail, killed Chief White Thunder and his old father after an incident involving the stealing of Chief White Thunder's young wife.

*Women hitching up the team to go
to the agency.*

Woman preparing a meal. The frame for a sweat lodge is behind the two men. A log house winter dance lodge is in the background.

Summer time tipi *camp. The bottoms of the* tipis *were folded up to give extra venti-lation and coolness. A sacred bundle, protectively wrapped, is on a pole in the foreground, signifying this is the* tipi *of a special person, warrior, or a chief.*

Gathering wood. An increasingly difficult chore in a country where firewood was scarce.

An Indian policeman's tipi home. Racks of meat are being dried into jerky. Sticks were stuck into the flat cuts of meat stretching it out, thus helping the drying process.

Nº9320 INDIAN HOME—DRYING BEEF.
PHOTO & COPYRIGHT BY J. A. ANDERSON. 1893

Louis Roubideaux with his wife and mother-in-law. He was the official interpreter for the agency.

*This type of settlement was called "pro-
gressive" and was usually built by the
People who cooperated with the white man
and who tried to adjust to the change
being imposed upon them.*

A typical home on the Rosebud in the later 1900s. The roof and floor were dirt. Note the ever-present tipi *close to the house.*

No. 245. MODERN INDIAN HOME. PHOTO. BY J. A. ANDERSON.

A prosperous home showing the women preparing the day's meal. This home was most likely the house of a man employed by the agency as a teamster or laborer.

*The snow on the ground does not prevent
the use of the* tipis. *These were usually
pitched facing the east to catch the early sun.*

A gathering at the office of the agent whose job was to handle all the problems of the People, no matter how big or small.

Meeting between Agent J. G. Wright and
a group of Indians, taken in 1896.

The commissary, a storehouse for all supplies, was surrounded by a stockade as a protection. The rations of flour, bacon, sugar, and coffee were given out once a month.

Herd of Texas cattle brought on the reservation by contractors and issued to the Indians as their beef ration.

*Texas cattle in the agency corral
waiting to be processed.*

*"We have heard the white man's buffalo
is here. We shall wait."*

"Gather, People, the meat is here. Come and see." In a short time, all the People were coming. (This photograph is attributed to W. R. Cross.)

No. 306. CATTLE TO BE ISSUED
PHOTO. BY J. A. ANDERSON.

In wagons, on horseback, on foot, they come. This made life good once again.

M 312. Scene At Beef Issue, Rosebud Agency S.D. Photo By J.A. Anderson.

Waiting for the beef issue at Cutmeat Creek.
The customary beef issue was once every
ten days. At times, however, this changed
to once a month.

Cattle had to be branded with the ID brand of the Indian Department. A hide without this mark of identification could not be sold or traded by the Indians.

*Two well-known old-time cowboys, Bob Dyer
and John Weiss, branding the beef-issue
cattle. The ID brand is shown quite clearly.*

Some beef was run through the slaughter-house at Cutmeat Creek.

Photo by J. A. Anderson. Slaughter & Issue House No. 317. Rosebud Agency S.D.

The amount of beef issued to each family
was determined by the number of people
in the family. This number was written
on a ration card which had to be presented
at the time of issue. This "up-to-date"
method of issuing meat prevented
the possibility of argument.

Cattle being slaughtered in the corrals. Distributing the meat in this manner meant that the People did their own butchering, cutting up the cattle where they fell.

49309 Killing Cattle for Indian issue.
Photo by J A Anderson.

The cattle, having been driven all the way
from Texas, were seldom in good shape.
Yet this was meat, and to the People,
the real food.

"The job is done. Now let the People come!"

Sometimes teams were used to drag the beef carcasses out to the ample spaces of the prairie where there was more room to work.

The oldest method of issuing beef was to turn the cows, one by one, onto the prairie where the men would run them down in a semblance of the old-time buffalo hunt. Here the warriors are getting their guns and horses ready for the chase.

Meat on the prairie.

"It is a pleasure to do this work. Our stomachs will be full. We shall feel good again!"

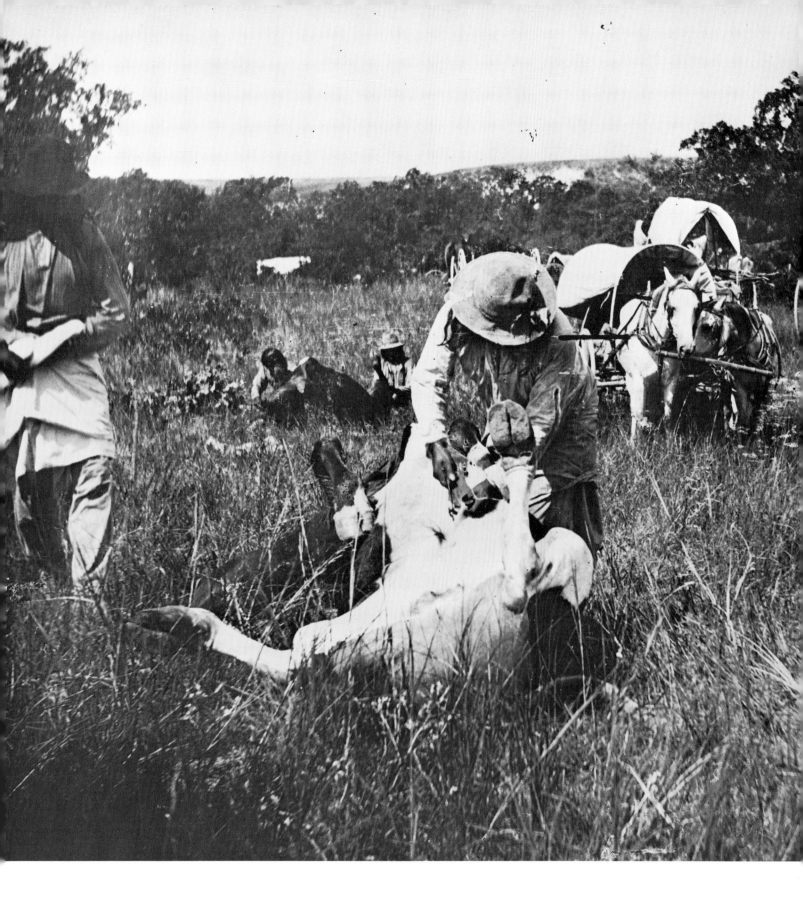

"Everybody pitch in . . ."

Bones will be cleaned and used. Nothing was ever wasted.

Indians Butchering Deer
313

Photo Copyright by JA Anderson 1893.

Women washing the beef entrails
(marrow guts) in the creek.
These were considered a delicacy.

"Load up. It's time to go and feast."

*"Brothers, once again we have red meat . . .
red, red, red meat!"*

A woman taking her share of meat home.
It shall be a good time!

No 318.
SIOUX SQUAW ON WAY HOME PHOTO BY J.A.ANDERSON
FROM BEEF ISSUE.

Preparing the meat in order that some of it may be preserved by making it into jerky or pemmican. Jerky was thinly sliced beef dried in the sun. Pemmican was dried meat pounded together with berries and fat. These were the old methods of preserving meat on the Plains.

"Meat is on the rack. Now it is time to visit and smoke." (Photograph is attributed to W. R. Cross.)

*Roasting beef entrails stuffed with meat
and fat. A Sioux delicacy!*

In the days before the horse, dogs were used
for transport. All camps had a large popu-
lation of dogs. Dog, the natural scavenger,
kept the camp sanitation to the minimum;
some were eaten as food, and
always they were respected as animals.
Many personal names of individuals
were based on the dog theme.

Never too young to ride a horse.

Young woman scurrying home with a load of wood.

*The travois, a time-honored method of
transport by which all the heavy gear of the
Plains People was moved. The horses pulling
the travois were ridden by women, as they
were responsible for the transport
of camp equipment.*

A group of young mothers with a travois that has a willow-branch over the seat. This kind of travois was used for the young children and very old people.

A woman preparing rawhide from which the parfleche was made. This was a suitcase-like case used for carrying anything from clothing to meat. The rawhide was scraped clean, stretched out, and painted in colored designs with stick brushes.

Two youngsters having a feast.

*The common method of using a blanket
to carry children when no cradle
was available.*

In the olden days before the white man's kettles, the Sioux, who had no pottery, used rawhide for food containers. Here an old woman is preparing a rawhide for use as a shallow bowl in which she will make pemmican. The chokeberries and wild plums will be placed in the bowl, pounded with a stone, and then mixed with the meat and fat.

Many hours were spent scraping the raw-hide. Removal of the excess fat and hair was the first step in the preparation of the skin.

Grandmother decorating a bag with bead-work. It was the creativity of this type of woman that produced the high degree of art so evident in the culture of the Brulé People.

A reservation funeral. The Indian police
are escorting the wagon and casket
to the cemetery.

The lamenting women.

Brulé graves on top of the ground.

N?249. INDIAN GRAVES, PHOTO. BY- J.A. ANDERSON.

*In the pre-reservation times the Plains
People buried their dead on scaffolds out on
the prairies. The dead, surrounded by their
possessions, were sewn in buffalo robes and
left to the elements of the land and sky.
In the early reservation period, caskets were
not available so the People would get large
trunks, place their loved ones in them, and
leave them on top of the ground. Interment
in the ground took place later only after
caskets became available.*

CHAPTER 5

CEREMONIAL LIFE

IN THE OLD CULTURE, religion was foremost in importance. There were no atheists; no one questioned the existence of God. With the advent of reservation life, accompanied by the white man's different religious factions and denominations who came prepared to enlighten the "spiritually poor," the People's need for the holy way of life and respect for the old religion were intensified instead of being diminished.

The Sun Dance was the most important ceremony of the Plains People. This dance was performed to fulfill the People's vows and to bring a good buffalo crop, and was a confirmation of the People's devotion to God.

The second most important ceremony that dealt with religion was the *Alowanpi* or Singing-Over Ceremony. It was held to honor the legendary white Buffalo Maiden who had brought the sacred pipe to the Sioux People. All the dances kept the People aware of the sacred purpose of life, and religion was on all sides of the old People's World.

It was only when devotion to the ancient beliefs failed to resurrect the old way of life that the beliefs began to lose ground. When the white man's religion did not fulfill promises, a movement of desperation called the Ghost Dance began. This movement grew out of the belief that Christ would come again. This time, however, He would come to the Indian and not to the white man who had crucified him. He would return the buffalo and the heart of the red man.

The leading priest of the Ghost Dance Movement was Short Bull, the younger brother of He Dog. This warrior, along with Kicking Bear, traveled to Nevada to get instructions for the Ghost Dance from its prophet Wovoka. The first dances were started at Iron Creek on the Rosebud Reservation late in the summer of 1890.

283

This movement, begun in such great hope, ended in a disaster. The Seventh Cavalry under Colonel Forsyth, in revenge for the Custer defeat, massacred men, women, and children at Wounded Knee, December 29, 1890. Chief Two Strike and other leaders attacked Pine Ridge Agency and a general insurrection resulted. General Nelson A. Miles had close to eight thousand troops in the area and assumed personal command. A day later, Chief Two Strike trapped the returning troops of the Seventh Cavalry on low ground near White Bird Camp, north of Pine Ridge Agency. Chief Two Strike, having the high ground, led the Seventh Cavalry into the situation with decoy warriors and once again, the Seventh faced defeat. The sudden appearance of Col. Guy V. Henry with his Negro Ninth Cavalry prevented additional bloodshed. Chief Two Strike, using great restraint and common sense, retired with his forces to his camp and was the last to surrender to General Miles on January 15, 1891.

General Miles stated, "They signed away a valuable portion of their reservation, and it is now occupied by white people, for which they received nothing. They understood that ample provision would be made for their support; instead, their supplies have been reduced and much of the time they have been living on half and two-thirds rations. Their crops, as well as the crops of white people, for two years have been almost a total failure. The disaffection is widespread, especially among the Sioux, while the Cheyennes have been on the verge of starvation and were forced to commit depredations to sustain life. These facts are beyond question, and the evidence is positive and sustained by thousands of witnesses."

After Wounded Knee, the People began a life of apathy and of survival on any terms. What old-time religion and ceremonials survived, were dearly cherished, along with the nostalgic pride that the Sioux People had accounted for themselves in the history of the West.

*A gathering of the People for a celebration
– this time, a "Give-Away." Tipi camps
of this kind were soon to be replaced
by the army-type wall tent camps.*

The presence of an army howitzer does not dampen the celebration spirit of the People. This was taken during the Ghost Dance Outbreak when the army tried to control as many camps as possible and keep order.

A couple going to a "Give-Away." They are taking the horse that they will give away publicly in honor of some relative. The man is wearing face paint and is carrying his fur-wrapped lance.

A "Give-Away" Ceremony. People came with gifts to be given away. These were piled up in the center of the camp and were given in thanks for a blessing bestowed upon them, such as the return of a loved one or the end of a sickness. Generosity has always been a Sioux virtue.

The lodge, with gifts for the children, and the preparation for a feast to honor the recipients.

*The Alowanpi or White Buffalo Maiden
Ceremony is the blessing of the children
to show the affection of the parents or the
relatives for the children. The children are
being painted with sacred red paint. This
ceremony was sometimes used as a Coming-
out Ceremony for the young virtuous girls.
The Sioux also called this
the Hunka Ceremony.*

The medicine man, ready for the blessing of food and gifts for the young maidens who are becoming women and now will be eligible for marriage.

No 301. WHITE BUFFALO
DANCE. SIOUX.
PHOTO. & COPYRIGHT. JAN. 1893
BY- J.A. ANDERSON.

Distribution of the blessed food to each young maiden. Each mouthful from the shallow bowl would be taken without touching the bowl with the hands. This insured them of a long and fruitful life. Following this ceremony the People feasted and everyone was happy.

Tipis *of the chiefs, taken at a Fourth of July*
celebration in 1911. The tipis *are decorated*
with paint and porcupine-quilled dangles.

*In the early days of the Rosebud Agency
the People staged this sham battle at day-
break of the Fourth of July Celebration
– a make-believe surprise on the agency.
A lot of yelling and shooting created happy
times for everyone – except the agent
who usually got nervous.*

Old-time winter dance lodge with a dirt roof. This type of lodge closely resembled the early pre-horse day earth lodge in design. Every community had its own dance lodge.

No. 281.
Sioux Indian Dance house.
Photo by— J A Anderson.

Young man coming to dance in the lodge.
Two shy belles, covered with blankets,
are sizing him up.

Spectators watch a dance lodge where many of the important ceremonies took place.

SIOUX INDIAN DANCE HOUSE

COPYRIGHT BY L A ANDERSON

*Left Hand Bull making ceremonial arrows,
some with stone heads. The sweat lodge
behind him was a structure of willow or
cottonwood branches which would be covered with buffalo hides. Stones were heated
outside and then brought inside. Water was
poured over the stones creating steam which
was to have soul-cleansing and healing
power. Practically every ceremony required
a sweat bath. This was a very important
part of the old-time religion. The white man's
religion did not require the civilized man
to take a bath. The sweat bath has survived
up to the present time among the old-timers.*

The camp crier, named Follows the Woman,
announcing the dances. The three-bladed
war club in his hand is an heirloom — a type
seldom seen at this time in the possession
of the old warriors.

*During many agency years the government
did not allow the Sioux People to partake
in or practice the Sun Dance, their most
important religious ceremony. It was condemned by the authorities as barbaric and
of an inciting nature against the government.
As an appeasement to the authorities the
People eliminated the practice of perforating
the breast and skin of the warrior dancers.
However, only men who had scars from
former Sun Dances could perform in this
agency version of the dance. Ropes were tied
under the arms in a simulated version
of the old pierced-skin performance.*

*Ceremonial Sun Dance Dog Feast. The dog
waiting to be killed will be cooked by the
ancient method. Heated stones will be thrown
into a water-filled container made from the
stomach of a cow. When the water boils
the dog is killed and put in to cook. The
center pole is covered with the People's
many offerings to God.*

Beef feast for the participants of the Sun Dance at the close of the ceremony.

*Five young men singled out for honors
by the People. The Southwestern Navajo
Chief's blankets, quite expensive at the time,
were gifts to the men from their relatives.*

High Bear starting a fire with flint and steel.
Kills Two, in his finest costume, is watch-
ing the procedure.

High Bear cooking meat by the ancient method of heating stones and throwing them into a beef-stomach container filled with water. High Bear lived until 1929.

Women at a feast roasting a dog.

Roasted dog was considered a delicacy. Ever since ancient times, the large dog population of the camps saved the People from starvation during the times when the Buffalo could not be found. By the reservation period the use of dogs as food was of a ceremonial nature rather than as plain food.

The warrior record of a man covering a ceremonial tipi. These records, first made on buffalo hides; then, in the reservation period, on anything that was available — canvas, paper, books — were of great importance to the old warriors as the documentation of their war deeds. These records were the finest examples of the Sioux art of drawing.

Chief High Hawk's ceremonial tipi. *The Brulé Sioux "Winter Count" is painted directly on the* tipi. *The use of the* tipi *as a surface for "Winter Count" drawings was most unusual. For that reason, this* tipi *was brought out only on very special occasions.*

*Summer tipi camp. Already some wall tents
are present – evidence of the changing times.*

A young Grass Dancer during the Ghost Dance Outbreak era. He is carrying a Grass Dance elk whistle and, suspended from a bandolier made from the dewclaws of a deer, he has his Sun Dance whistle and his Sun Dance lariat by which he was tied to the center pole at some previous Sun Dance ceremony. Since the government had issued restriction on all types of dances even as late as 1915, this young man would have been considered very unreliable by the agency authorities as he was plainly a warrior.

The Grass Dance, one of the most popular dances for the warriors. It is sometimes called the Omaha Dance as the Omaha People possibly originated the dance long ago.

This dance has a lot of action. The costumes were usually lightweight and bustles were worn. The warriors tried to outdo each other in the intricacies of the steps.

The man in front is simulating a war action of his past. Wooden guns were quite popular with the old warriors as a symbol of war actions.

Grass Dancers re-enacting war deeds.

Resting dancers, ready for the next round, in front of Louis Roubideaux's big house.

Grass Dancers in full regalia, mostly young men. Several have Dog Soldier Society collars with mirrors — a mark of warriors.

Group of Sioux in War Paint

Resting dancers with chiefs
present in the group.

Woman's Dance with men singers and drummers in the center. Women did not dance in the "white man" couple fashion.

N° 289. SQUAW DANCE
PHOTO. & COPYRIGHT.
By—
J.A.ANDERSON.
1893.

Full circle of dancing women taken in 1893.
The women formed a circle and danced
with a slow side step, the entire
circle moving together.

Kills Two, a Brulé medicine man, painting
a history record called the "Big Missouri
Winter Count." It began in 1796 and ended
in 1926. Each picture painted on the skin
represented a year and was a picture of some-
thing that, to the Brulé, was the most out-
standing event of that particular year.

CHAPTER 6

The photographer: John Anderson

JOHN ANDERSON was born in Sweden, March 25, 1869, and came out to western Nebraska in 1884, where his father took up a homestead in the Fort Niobrara District.

When he was seventeen he went to work for a photographer, W. R. Cross, one of the first trained photographers on the Plains. From this man, young Anderson learned the business of photography. Soon he had his own studio at Fort Niobrara.

In May, 1889, the Sioux Land Commissioners along with General Crook, came to Rosebud Agency to induce the Brulé Sioux People to sign their lands away. John Anderson went along as a photographer for General Crook.

At Rosebud Agency, John Anderson found the color he had been seeking. There he met the agency trader, C. P. Jordan, who was quite a colorful character. Jordan was married to Chief Red Cloud's daughter and had a great deal of experience in the Indian trade, having obtained his trader's license in the early 1880s. Jordan offered the young man a job as bookkeeper and manager of the trading post at Rosebud Agency. Anderson was only too happy to accept, as this gave him the opportunity to make a living and pursue his photography interests as well.

John Anderson worked in the trading post while his employer, now billed as Colonel Jordan, toured the country with his own Wild West Show—his prime interest. When the trading post could no longer sustain the losses incurred by the show, Jordan sold out to the Hornby Brothers of Valentine, Nebraska. These experienced merchants appreciated young Anderson's talents and offered him a partnership in the trading post, now re-named The Jordan Mercantile Company. All the goods and supplies for the post had to be hauled by wagons from the railroad at Valentine, Nebraska—a distance of close to forty miles.

John Anderson spent forty-two years as a trader at the Rosebud Agency. He gathered a substantial collection of Indian artifacts which were later acquired by the Sioux Museum in Rapid City, South Dakota, where he spent three years as a director after he retired from the trading post. In 1939, he moved to Atascadero, California, maintaining a home there until his death in 1948.

John Anderson left a legacy of 400 glass-plate negatives, a unique record of the early reservation period and certainly the finest record of the Brulé People. Following his death in 1948, his old friend, Carl H. Parlasca, the originator of the Hiawatha Pageant in Elgin, Illinois, was able to secure the glass-plate negatives from Anderson's widow. Through Parlasca's efforts the life work of John Anderson was finally brought to the attention of the public. That the glass plates survived their adventurous life – after being in basements, attics, outside porches – this is the miracle.

Because men such as John Anderson did exist and cared so compassionately, the early story of the West and its people will live for the future generations – a glimpse from our past – a past long since gone.

John Anderson in his first studio at Fort Niobrara, Nebraska, taken in 1888.

John Anderson with Old Harney, General Harney's scout, taken in 1888.

ACKNOWLEDGMENTS

TO ALL THE SIOUX FRIENDS, many since deceased, who provided the inspiration that has made this volume possible. On the Rosebud Reservation: Stephen Spotted Tail, John Face, Ida White Cow Killer, Adam Bordeaux, George Goodbreast, Nellie Meynard, Silas Yellow Boy, Lillian Bear Heels, Lorraine Metcalf, Alice Fish, Joe Beads, Joe Black Tomahawk, Jim High Hawk, Kate Little Thunder.

On the Pine Ridge Reservation: Frank Kicking Bear, George Respects Nothing, Henry Weasel, Charles Little Hawk, Matthew Eagle Heart, James Holy Eagle, Anna Pretty Bird, Angelique Fire Thunder, Philip Blue Bird, Andrew Fools Crow, Ed Iron Cloud, Cecelia Jumping Bull, Wallace Little Finger, Lone Elk.

On the Cheyenne River Reservation: Jake Hollow Horn, Billie War Bonnet, Grant Iron Lightning, Claude Iron Hawk, Moses Circle Bear.

On the Standing Rock Reservation: One Elk, Judge Frank B. Zahn, Cecelia One Bull, Sidney Eagle Shell, Spotted Elk.

At Wood Mountain, Saskatchewan, Canada: George Wounded Horse.

The Smithsonian Institution, Bureau of American Ethnology, for the Chief Spotted Tail photographs, pages 35, 37, 39, 41 and 49.

The State of South Dakota Historical Society for the photograph of Chief Spotted Tail and his children, page 43.

The U. S. Department of Interior Indian Arts and Crafts Board, Sioux Indian Museum and Crafts Center, Rapid City, South Dakota, for the photographs of John Anderson, pages 361 and 363.

Gilbert R. Wenger, Park Archaeologist, Mesa Verde National Park, Colorado, who devoted many hours in his dark room enlarging and printing over eighty photographs from the glass-plate negatives.

Miss Ella Lebow, Director of the Sioux Indian Museum and Crafts Center, Rapid City, South Dakota, who has been generous in providing photographs and information about John Anderson.

Jack R. Williams, United States Park Service, Nez Perce National Park, Idaho, for his cooperation and the use of the glass-plate negatives of the John Anderson Collection.

Jean S. Dyck, my wife, for endless hours of patience and work.

RECOMMENDED READING

FOR THOSE PEOPLE interested in making history come alive once again, here is a suggested list of books which deal with the detailed history of the Brulé Sioux and others who were involved in the events of the time related to the photographs in this book.

George E. Hyde, *Spotted Tail Folk,* University of Oklahoma Press, 1961.

George E. Hyde, *A Sioux Chronicle,* University of Oklahoma Press, 1956.

George E. Hyde, *Red Cloud Folk,* University of Oklahoma Press, 1937.

14th Annual Report of the Bureau of Ethnology, 1892-93, Part 2.

Teton Sioux Music, Bulletin 61, Bureau of American Ethnology, 1918.

THIS BOOK WAS DESIGNED
BY ROBERT JACOBSON
AND SET IN HERMAN ZAPF'S ALDUS.
IT WAS PRINTED ON POLOMA MATTE
AT NORTHLAND PRESS
AND BOUND BY ROSWELL BINDERY.